MASTERING GRAMMAR & COMPOSITION

BOOK 4

Robert Bellarmine

BPI INDIA PVT LTD

BPI INDIA PVT LTD
F-213/A, Ground Floor,
Old Mehrauli Badarpur Road,
Lado Sarai, New Delhi - 110030 (India)
Tel: +91-11-43394300-99, E-mail: sales@bpiindia.com

ISBN: 978817693054-3

The views expressed and the material provided in this book are solely those of the author and presented by the publisher in good faith. The publisher is in no way responsible for the same.

Publisher's Note

Why This New Series? Experienced primary teachers have noticed three major gaps in the materials available today for teaching grammar. Child-friendly exercises are scarce. Genuine grammar games are almost nil. Very little is done to lay the foundation for teaching formal grammar by raising learners' awareness of language form at the basic level of sounds, letter and words. Mastering Grammar and Composition series fills these gaps. This series comprises Books 1-5.

Book 1 and Book 2—meant for standards I and II respectively—are designed to:

- Build the foundation for learning grammar by raising learners' awareness of the formal features of language at the elementary levels of sounds, letters and words. Language Awareness section, a special feature in these books, deals with these less complex and less abstract aspects of grammar;

- Eliminate learners' fear of grammar by focusing on elementary aspects of grammar and using interesting techniques.

Books 3-5, meant for standards III – V, focus on formal grammar, dealing with language awareness only marginally. In helping children apply grammar to real or realistic situations, compose sentences, and correct sentences, these books are similar to, but more extensive than, Books I and II.

How Different from Workbooks: These Mastering Grammar and Composition books are significantly different in method from other workbooks. Techniques such as those in Grammar and I, Grammar in Quotes, Grammar Games and Grammar Activities are unique to the Grammar and Composition series.

Syllabus Contents: In the matter of the selection of grammatical content or syllabus items, the books do overlap in parts. But the purpose has been to reinforce and consolidate some grammatical items by repeating and 'spiralling' them.

Structure of Lessons: A lesson consists of four major sections/stages.

- The Preliminary Section introduces a grammatical item or prepares students/ teachers for an exercise or activity.
- The Exercise or Activity section helps the students use the target language or grammatical item in a game or activity or exercise.
- The Definition Section sums up the concepts and rules introduced in the lesson. It also attempts to help the learner understand and remember it.

- The Composition Section consolidates the learning of various grammatical items and enables the learner to use them in a more sustained and extended way than in sentence level exercise.

Caters to Different Types of Teachers/Learners: We have mixed Activity with Exercise, the Modern with the Traditional, the Learner-Centred with the Subject-Centred approaches to accommodate all types of teachers and learners.

Revives Some Traditional Practices: We have also dared to revive some traditional practices such as memorising and learning of rules, definitions and labels.

Reduces Before-Class Preparation: Even the best teacher struggles to find the time needed to teach the large and mixed classes of today. A conscious effort has been made in the series to make little or no demand on teachers' before-class time preparation or on sophisticated knowledge of grammar or modern classroom techniques. Further, all the information and instruction teachers need to set up activities/exercises have been included in the body of the unit for immediate reference.

Instant-Aid Footnotes: For immediate and easy reference, all the explanations necessary to tell the teacher why certain items have been included or how an exercise or activity can be varied/simplified have been included in the footnote at the bottom of the page.

To the Teacher: We believe that a good textbook should not make teaching dull or difficult. We have tried to make teaching both easy and enjoyable through these books. At the same time, we have provided for the teacher's professional development by choosing new games and activities and by including informative explanations and instructions in the footnotes.

To the Parent: Increasingly, the school and the home reciprocity are being appreciated by teachers, principals, management and parents. Further, because of keen competition and the critical importance of academic success, classroom teaching is often supplemented by parents and private tutors. Some schools organise such supplementary teaching themselves. In many parts of the book, therefore, this involvement of parents and supplementary tutors outside the classroom is exploited. This is accomplished through 'collaborative exercises' that require parents and others in the child's immediate environment to work with them.

The Multi-Party Partnership in Education: We have entered the Indian education scene at a time when the publisher's role as a partner in imparting quality education is appreciated. In recognition of this important role, we have endeavoured to make our books educationally worthwhile to all users.

Contents

WORD BUILDING

Prefixes ─────────────────────────────

Try and divide the following words into two parts. You will notice that one part is a full word.

Example: undo   un + do

Here 'do' is a full word,

'un' is a part of the word.

	Part of the Word	+	Full Word
Example: untie	un	+	tie
1. unwise	_____	+	_____
2. unpleasant	_____	+	_____
3. unsatisfactory	_____	+	_____
4. discomfort	_____	+	_____
5. disobey	_____	+	_____
6. impossible	_____	+	_____
7. impatient	_____	+	_____
8. imperfect	_____	+	_____
9. unlucky	_____	+	_____
10. inaccurate	_____	+	_____
11. incorrect	_____	+	_____
12. insincere	_____	+	_____
13. unhappy	_____	+	_____

The parts of the words 'un-', 'dis-', 'im-' and 'in-' are called 'prefixes'. Can you guess why they are called 'pre-' fixes? Do you remember the meaning of 'pre' in 'preposition'?

Which of the following is the meaning of 'pre-'? (Ring) the meaning.
Always, before, after, central

 Points to Remember

A prefix is a letter or a group of letters added to the front of a word to change its meaning.

a. By adding 'un-' to a word, you can create its opposite:
   Form the opposites of the following by adding 'un-.'

   happy   x _____

   wise   x _____

   loving   x _____

   natural   x _____

   known   x _____

b. By adding 'dis-' to a word, you can create its opposite.
   Form the opposites of the following by adding 'dis-'.

   prove   x _____

   obey   x _____

   like   x _____

   please   x _____

   connect   x _____

c. By adding 'im-' to a word, you can create its opposite.
   Form the opposites of the following by adding 'im-'.

   possible x _____

   polite   x _____

   patient   x _____

   proper   x _____

   perfect   x _____

d. By adding 'in-' to a word, you can create its opposite.
   Form the opposites of the following by adding 'in-'.

   correct   x _____

   direct   x _____

   decent   x _____

   dependent   x _____

   expensive   x _____

e. The meaning of the following sentences will change if you use the opposite
   of the underlined words. Add the necessary prefixes to form the opposites.
   Rewrite the sentences in the space provided.

1. Take this magical drink. You will become <u>visible</u>.

   _____

2. Nothing is <u>possible</u> with hard work.

_____

3. Some diseases are <u>curable</u>.

_____

4. Some kings are <u>wise</u>.

_____

5. Some people are <u>lucky</u>.

_____

6. This eraser is <u>common</u>.

_____

Suffixes

Suffix '-ly'

Look at the following pairs of sentences. In all the sentences marked 'a', the underlined words are adjectives. Because they add to the meaning of _____ (verbs, nouns, adverbs)

Look at the sentences marked 'b'. All the underlined words in them are adverbs. Because they add to the meaning of_____ (verbs, nouns, adverbs)

1. a. This is the <u>right</u> answer.

   b. You were <u>rightly</u> angry.

2. a. This is a <u>real</u> story.

   b. This story <u>really</u> happened.

3. a. This is a complete essay.

   b. This is <u>completely</u> wrong.

4. a. This is a wonderful statue.

   b. This statue is <u>wonderfully</u> made.

5. a. I don't like <u>slow</u> action.

   b. You are acting <u>slowly</u>.

Points to Remember

Adjectives modify the meanings of nouns. And adverbs modify the meanings of verbs.

Most adverbs end in '-ly'. You can change many adjectives into adverbs by adding the suffix '-ly'.

You can turn adjectives into adverbs by simply adding the Suffix '-ly'.

Example:

slow   slowly

real   really

right   rightly

complete   completely

Spelling Rule: 1

Suppose the last letter of an adjective is 'y'. To turn it into an adverb, first change 'y' into 'i'. Then add the suffix '-ly'.

happy   happi   +   ly   happily

easy   easi   +   ly   easily

Now turn the following adjectives into their adverbs:

speedy, lazy, cozy

Spelling Rule: 2

Suppose an adjective ends in 'le'. To turn it into an adverb, first remove the 'le' and add the suffix '-ly'.

idle ——— idly   noble ——— nobly

Now turn the following adjectives into their adverbs:

able, probable, single, possible, gentle

Suffix '-tion' and '-ion'

Look at the following pairs of sentences and the words underlined in them.

1. a. Reduce the price.

   b. We do not allow any <u>reduction</u>.

2. a. Produce more food.

   b. We must encourage more food <u>production</u>.

Spelling Rule: 3

1. When the verbs end in '-ce', first drop the final 'e' and then add '-tion'.

Fill up the following blanks:

verbs	noun
reduce	_____
produce	_____

Spelling Rule: 4

2. When the verbs end in '-se' or '-te', first omit the final 'e'. Then add '-ion' to produce the noun.

   Study the following example:

   confuse ⎯⎯⎯⎯⎯⎯→ confusion

   rotate ⎯⎯⎯⎯⎯⎯→ rotation

Create more nouns from the following verbs by adding '-tion' or '-ion'

Verb		Noun
revise	–	_____
rotate	–	_____
relate	–	_____
deduce	–	_____
promote	–	_____
duplicate	–	_____
devote	–	_____
supervise	–	_____

These verbs are turned into their nouns by the addition of '-ion'.

Create your own nouns from the following verbs:

act	⎯⎯→	_____
exhibit	⎯⎯→	_____
connect	⎯⎯→	_____
insert	⎯⎯→	_____

protect   ————→   _____

subtract   ————→   _____

Suffix '-ment'

Yet another useful suffix is '-ment'. This turns verbs into nouns. Study the following pairs of sentences. The first sentence of each pair contains a verb. The second sentence contains the noun form of the verb.

1. a. Please arrange for a flower show.

    b. Please make the arrangement for a flower show.

2. a. Improve your handwriting, Peter.

    b. Aim at the improvement of your handwriting, Peter.

3. a. We all fulfil our wishes.

    b. We all want the fulfilment of our wishes.

Make the noun forms from the following verbs using '-ment'.

manage   ————→   _____

postpone   ————→   _____

govern   ————→   _____

imprison   ————→   _____

amaze   ————→   _____

discourage   ————→   _____

encourage   ————→   _____

develop   ————→   _____

judge   ————→   _____

ACTIVITY

Thomas Alva Edison

Step One: Your teacher will read the following story twice. As you listen, try to write down the words with the common suffixes, '-ment', '-ly', '-ion' and '-tion' in the given table. Do not worry about the spelling.

"This story is about the famous inventor, Edison. He is known for the invention of the electric bulb. He was good at keen observation even as a child. One day, he watched a goose sitting on its eggs. It turned the eggs. Then it sat on them. It turned them again. Then it started going around the eggs. Edison watched all these movements.

Then one of the eggs cracked. Edison was filled with amazement. A small, tiny head stuck out. Edison jumped at this action of the chick. In great excitement, he ran out.

He picked up a handful of straw. He shaped it into a nest. He saw a basketful of eggs in a corner. He carefully selected two eggs. He then sat on them. He patiently sat on them for hours. He stroked them warmly. He repeated the actions of the mother goose. He then eagerly waited for the eggs to crack.

No egg cracked. No chick stuck its neck out. Edison was filled with disappointment. His mother explained that only birds knew how to hatch eggs. He made a decision then to make a hatching machine."

'-ment'	'-ly'	'-tion'	'-ion'
Example: movements			

Step Two: Now read the story silently. Mark the words with the suffixes '-ment', '-ly', '-tion' and '-ion' in the story. Complete the table. Check the spellings of the words you have already written and correct them if they are wrong.

Step Three: Now turn the words ending in '-ment', '-tion' and '-ion' into their verbs. Turn the words ending in '-ly' into their adjectives. Write the words you have made in the appropriate columns.

Verbs	Adjectives
Example: invent	careful

Grammar in Quotes

Study the following proverb. Spot the opposite with a prefix.
Copy it three times in the blanks after the proverb.
'What is done cannot be undone.'

_____

_____

_____

Of the following mistakes that one may commit, which are the ones that can be rectified?

taking the life of an animal.

cutting or breaking the branch of a tree.

Both or none

Now try to memorise the proverb. Learn one word at a time. Do not skip a step before getting the word of that step right. Getting it right is as important as doing it fast.

Fill in the missing words in the proverb:

"What is done cannot be undone." (6 words)

"What is _____ cannot be undone."

"What is _____ cannot be _____."

"_____ is _____ cannot be _____."

"_____ is _____ cannot _____ _____"

"_____ _____ _____ _____ _____ _____." (6 words)

COUNTABLE AND UNCOUNTABLE NOUNS

Revision: Nouns and Articles ─────────

1. What is a noun?
   A noun is a _____ word. It _____ a person, a place, an animal or a thing.
2. Ring the nouns in the following sentences:
   Computers are now made in India.
   Some boys run fast.
   Some girls run fast, too.
3. Underline the articles in the following sentences:
   An apple a day keeps the doctor away.
   A bird in hand is better than two in the bush.
   The dog wags its tail.

Using numbers from one to ten, count the following. Fill up the blanks with the correct number.

Change the singular into the plural noun, wherever necessary.

Example:

four bananas

_____ rose

_____ rice

_____ salt

_____ pencils

_____ cats

_____ monkey

_____ penguins

_____ water

15

Were you able to count the things in all the pictures above?

Yes/No

> **Points to Remember**
>
> Certain things cannot be counted at all. Example: milk, water, oil.
> Certain things are not usually counted, because they cannot be easily counted. Example: rice, wheat, sugar, sand.
> The words naming such things are called 'uncountable nouns'.
> Certain other things are easily counted or usually counted.
> Example: pencils, boys, dresses, houses, bananas.
> The words naming such things are called 'countable nouns'.

Fill up the blanks with uncountable nouns. Choose the words for the blanks from list given below:

gold, paper, silver, wood, graphite, wool, cotton, lead, plastic, rubber, silk, wheat, milk

Is India really a poor country? Study the following facts:

1. Most Indians use _____ to make ornaments. Only some Indians, for example, the Lambadis of Andhra Pradesh use _____ to make ornaments.

2. India produces enough food. Its stock of _____ and rice is excellent. It produces a lot of _____ because of its high cattle population.

3. Using straw, grass and wood, India produces its own _____. It produces pencils using _____ and _____.

4. India produces enough _____ to make sweaters for its people. In Kancheepuram, Benaras and other places Indians use _____ to make sarees. In most places, _____ is used to make sarees. But sarees made from _____ are very expensive and very beautiful.

5. Before _____ was invented, furniture was made of _____ and steel all over the world. Now we have plastic chairs, plastic tables and plastic stands. India produces enough _____ to make these things. Using _____, we also make tyres and tubes. Like Malaysia, India grows a lot of rubber trees.

Rule 1: Indefinite articles 'a' and 'an' cannot be used before uncountable nouns. The sentences marked with a cross (X) are incorrect because they go against this rule. The sentences marked with a tick (✓) are the correct ones.

Example: 1

Give me <u>a</u> <u>paper</u>.   X

Give me <u>a</u> <u>sheet</u> <u>of</u> <u>paper</u>. ✓

Give me <u>a</u> <u>piece</u> <u>of</u> <u>paper</u>. ✓

Example: 2

I have <u>an</u> <u>information</u>.   X

I have <u>a</u> <u>piece</u> <u>of</u> <u>information</u>.

Rule 2: Quantity words 'few', 'a few', 'many' and 'several' cannot be used before uncountable nouns. Uncountable nouns do not have a plural form. The sentences marked with a cross (X) are wrong because they do not follow this rule. The sentences marked with a tick (✓) are the correct ones.

We sell many wheats.   X

We sell many varieties of wheat. ✓

We sell a lot of wheat. ✓

You have only a few rices.   X

You have only a little rice. ✓

You have only a few varieties of rice.   ✓

Rich people have many money.   X

Rich people have much money. ✓

Rich people have a lot of money. ✓

I drink a lot of milks.   X

I drink a lot of milk. ✓

I drink several glasses of milk. ✓

I drink a several litres of milk. ✓

Rule 3: The plural demonstrative pronouns 'these' and 'those' cannot be used before uncountable nouns. Uncountable nouns do not have a plural form. The sentences marked with a tick (✓) are the correct ones.

Your uniform is made of these cloths.   X

Your uniform is made of these types of cloth. ✓

Your uniform is made of these pieces of cloth. ✓

Your uniform is made of these sheets of cloth. ✓

These sceneries in the picture are not so good.   X

These scenery in the picture is not so good. ✓

Those sceneries were more beautiful.   X

That scenery in the picture was more beautiful. ✓

I will give you a few news.   X

To become strong, eat many wheats.   X

I saw these sceneries in the Himalayas.   X

This uniform is made of several cloths.   X

But indefinite articles ('a' and 'an'), some quantity words ('few', 'a few', 'many' and 'several') and the plural demonstrative pronouns ('these' and 'those') are often placed before countable nouns. This is why the following sentences are correct:

I have several books at home.

These vegetables look fresh and green.

I have borrowed a pencil from my friend.

I saw four pictures in her house.

> **To the teacher:** Some nouns are both countable and uncountable. But the meaning of the countable noun is slightly different from the meaning of the uncountable noun.
>
> 'Wood' in its uncountable sense refers to the material from which paper or furniture is made.
>
> 'Wood' in the countable sense refers to an area filled with trees but smaller than a forest. Example: "The woods are lovely, dark and deep."
>
> 'Wood' in the countable sense can also mean a particular variety of the material. Example: "This cupboard is made of a hard wood called teak."
> "Pine is a soft wood."

 Points to Remember

Indefinite articles ('a' and 'an'), quantity words ('few', 'a few', 'many' and 'several') and plural demonstrative pronouns ('these' and 'those') cannot be used before uncountable nouns.

Common Mistakes

Six of the following ten sentences are incorrect. Four of the ten are correct. Put a tick mark (✓) against the correct ones.

Look at the incorrect sentences and see if:

(a) the uncountable nouns in them are used in the plural form

(b) quantity words, indefinite articles, numerals, and plural demonstrative pronouns occur before the uncountable nouns.

Rewrite the sentences after correcting the mistakes in them.

1. All India Radio gives us many news.

   _____

2. We have five chairs at home.

   _____

3. They use many furnitures.

   _____

4. He eats two mangoes a day.

   _____

5. I eat different fruits in different seasons.

   _____

6. Some vegetarians eat chicken.

   _____

7. These five fishes are of the same kind.

   _____

8. Our uniforms are made of two cloths.

   _____

9. I have thirty jewelleries, including these five rings and bangles.

   _____

10. The exhibition gives many informations.

    _____

> **To the Teacher:** 'Fruit' and 'fish', like 'chicken', are common and useful words. But their grammatical behaviour is tricky. Their plural form 'fruits' and 'fishes' can be used when referring to different kinds of fruit or fish. But the singular form is commonly used, and therefore, it is safer to use the singular form than the plural form.
> 'Chicken' is countable when it refers to the bird. It is uncountable when it refers to its meat.

If words referring to quantity and number cannot go with uncountable nouns, then how do we express their quantity?

Look at the pictures shown below. The quantity of cloth in picture 1 is not the same as the quantity of cloth in picture 2 or in picture 3. Cloth is an uncountable noun. How can we express the three quantities? How can we express the differences?

Answer: There is only one piece of cloth in picture 1.

There are two pieces of cloth in picture 2.

There are three pieces of cloth in picture 3.

To show the quantity of uncountable words some other words like 'piece of' are placed before them. The following is a useful list:

Quantity Words	Uncountable Nouns (Solids)
a piece of two pieces of several pieces of	news, information, knowledge, advice, work, furniture, cloth, paper, baggage, luggage, bread, cake
a sheet of two sheets of many sheets of	paper
one slice of two slices of a few slices of	bread cake
one bar of	soap, chocolate
a kilogram of two kilograms of	meat, chicken, mutton rice, wheat, salt, sugar
a glass of one glass of two glasses of	water milk
a cup of two cups of	tea coffee
a litre of one litre of two litres of	oil milk water kerosene petrol

Ping-Pong

To the Teacher: This is just like the game of Ping-Pong. The ball passes from one to the other.

Step One: A list of nouns is given below. The countable and the uncountable nouns are mixed in the list.

You call out a noun from the list and your partner will have to say 'countable' or 'uncountable'.

Now your partner will give you a noun from the list and it is your turn to say 'countable' or 'uncountable'.

Continue till one of you makes a mistake or breaks the chain. Stop when all the words from the list are used up.

Step two: Continue the activity with a slight variation. When you give a noun to your partner he/she will have to do two things:

1. Identify whether the noun is countable or uncountable.

2. Then repeat the word you have just said with a correct quantity word such as articles or numerals before it.

Example: 1

You: Biscuit

Your Partner: Countable, two biscuits/a biscuit/many biscuits

Example: 2

You: Tea

Your Partner: Uncountable, a cup of tea/two cups of tea

Word List

wheat	milk	cloth	clothes
apple	meat	chicken	fish
news	sugar	salt	apples
rice	blood	fruit	tree
pencils	boy	girl	school
information	shirt	lesson	word
oil	water	paint	polish

Scoring: 1 point for saying countable/uncountable correctly.

1 point for using the correct quantity word before it.

Articles Before Uncountable Nouns

When uncountable nouns have to have a general meaning, they can be used without the definite article 'the'.

Example:

Water is a useful liquid.

Many people in Asia eat rice.

Most people in the West eat wheat.

Gold is a precious metal.

Cotton is nature's gift.

If you have to refer to a particular kind of thing, then the definite article 'the' is placed before the uncountable noun.

Example:

The wheat from Punjab is different from the wheat from Madhya Pradesh.

The rice from Dehradun is better than the rice from Vellore.

The cotton from Egypt has long fibre.

We like the international programme of FM Radio.

COMPOSITION

Fill up the following blanks with 'a' 'an' 'the' or 'X'. Put 'X' if none of the three articles can be used.

_____ paper was first made about five hundred years ago. Before that some people wrote with _____ iron rod on slabs made of clay. _____ paper you are using now is made from _____ wood. _____ paper used to make currency notes is of a very special kind. _____ ink too was invented about five hundred years ago. _____ ink we put into _____ ball point pen is different from _____ ink we put into _____ fountain pen. Invisible inks are made from _____ oil extracted from a plant. _____ indelible ink is _____ ink that cannot be erased. Ink is very useful because it helps us spread knowledge. This is why _____ famous writer has said, "_____ drop of _____ ink can make millions think".

COMPOSITION

Imagine that you are in the furniture shop shown in the picture below:

FURNITURE SHOP

Describe four things in the shop to your friend. While describing you can state:

1. the name of the object

2. its shape and size

3. its position in the shop

4. the material it is made of

Example:

There is a tall ladder in the shop. It is in the right hand corner of the shop. It is made of wood.

Now begin:

1. There is/a/are/a few/many/several _____ in the shop

_____

_____

2. _____

_____

_____

3. _____

_____

_____

4. _____

_____

_____

Grammar in Quotes

Study the following proverb. Listen to the teacher's explanation of its meaning.

"Blood is thicker than water."

1. Now, underline the two nouns in it.

   Are they both countable or uncountable?

2. Learn the proverb by heart.

   "Blood is thicker than water." (5 words)

   "Blood _____ thicker than water."

   "Blood _____ thicker _____ water."

   "Blood _____ _____ _____ water."

   "Blood _____ _____ _____ _____."

   "_____ _____ _____ _____ _____." (5 words)

PREPOSITIONS

Revision

1. Ring the preposition in the following list of words.
   under, the, your, put

2. Which word in the following sentence is a preposition? Underline the preposition. "Don't leave your shoes on the sofa!"

3. What is the meaning of 'pre-' in 'preposition'?
   Circle your answer.
   always, before, after, now

Have you seen toadstools? Look at the following picture of this interesting plant. Here is a poem on the birth of this plant.

First listen to the teacher reading it. Try to understand the story. Now you read the poem silently. Tick (✓) all the prepositions in the poem.

The One-Legged Stool

Long ago <u>in</u> Fairyland
    There lived a clumsy toad;
(He had a cottage, small and brown,
    Along the Dreamland Road.)
He grew so <u>very</u>, very fat,
    That suddenly one day,
When he was sitting in his chair,
    He felt the leg give way.
(And down he fell <u>upon</u> the floor,
    And lay there, scared to death;
Then up he got, and <u>on</u> his bed
    Sat down to get his breath.)
'I'll make myself a stool,' he said,
    'With one leg, strong <u>and</u> straight;
(And when I sit <u>upon</u> that stool,
    Perhaps 'twill bear my weight.')
He made it with a round <u>top</u>,
    And one stout leg below;
(Said he, 'That's just the thing I want,
    'Twill suit me well, I know.')

By Enid Blyton
From *Let's Enjoy Poetry*

1. a. How many prepositions did you spot? _____

To the Teacher: There are 6 prepositions in the poem.

b. Look at the seven words underlined in the poem. Three of them are not prepositions. Circle only the prepositions.

2. Group the prepositions that are underlined in the following sentences. Put them in two groups and write them in the table given below:

a. My books are <u>on</u> the table and my bag is <u>on</u> the floor.

b. Give the chocolate <u>to</u> Ron and the cake <u>to</u> Ken.

c. Don't leave the clothes <u>in</u> the washing machine but put them <u>into</u> a bucket.

d. Take the ice cream <u>from</u> Rick and give it <u>to</u> Angelina.

e. Some pupils walk <u>from</u> the school <u>to</u> the bus stop.

f. The cat always sleeps <u>under</u> the table.

g. In the English alphabet 'y' is <u>between</u> 'x' and 'z'.

Prepositions of Position	Prepositions of Direction
_____	_____
_____	_____
_____	_____
_____	_____
_____	_____

3. Fill the blanks in the following text choosing the correct preposition from the list.

The policemen and a thief are standing _____ the top shelf. On the next shelf, a frog is sitting _____ a baby frog. Dinky, the clever mouse, is hiding _____ the shelf. Kitty, the cat, is sitting _____ a basket.

Prepositions: in, on, with, under

Prepositions of Time

Some prepositions are connected with time.

Study the prepositions in the following sentences:

Our school is closed <u>on</u> Sundays.

Some shops are closed <u>on</u> Tuesdays.

The cartoon show starts <u>at</u> 7 p.m.

We switch on our lights <u>at</u> 6 p.m.

India became free <u>in</u> 1947.

I was born <u>in</u> 2001.

We celebrate Deepavali <u>in</u> October or November.

Their summer vacation begins <u>in</u> May.

We reach the school <u>before</u> 8 a.m.

We leave the school <u>after</u> 3 p.m.

Fill up the blanks in the following sentences with prepositions of time.

1. All Fools' Day is celebrated _____ 1 April.
2. The Mumbai–Delhi Rajdhani Express leaves _____ 5 p.m.
3. Penicillin was discovered _____ 1928.
4. The first T.V was made _____ 1927.
5. India got its freedom _____ 12 o'clock midnight.
6. In some parts of the world the sun sets very early, _____ 3 p.m.
7. In some other parts of the world the sun sets very late, _____ 8 p.m.
8. We celebrate Christmas _____ December.
9. The first atom bomb exploded _____ 8.15 a.m. _____ 6 August _____ the year 1945.
10. India won the World Cup in hockey _____ 1975.

Grammar and I

Complete the following table. You may consult people at home.

S.No	Question	Answer Preposition	Answer Time Expression
1.	When does your mother get up in the morning?	_____	_____
2.	When do you get up?	_____	_____
3.	When were you born?	_____	_____
4.	When did you join this school? Mention the month.	_____	_____
5.	When do you start for school in the morning?	_____	_____
6.	When do we celebrate our Independence Day?	_____	_____
7.	When do we celebrate our Republic Day?	_____	_____
8.	Independence day comes _____ Republic day.	_____	_____
9.	Your birthday comes_____ your Father's birthday.	_____	_____
10.	When do you not go to school? Use one of the names of days.	_____	_____

Common Mistakes

Put the correct prepositions in the place of the incorrect ones:

1. The child sat in the stool.

   _____

2. I go to school from the school bus.

   _____

3. I will meet you on 5 o'clock.

   _____

4. There is too much hair in his face.

   _____

5. Place these coloured glasses in your eyes. You can then see the eclipse clearly.

   _____

6. I want to see a new English play in the theatre.

   _____

COMPOSITION

Look at the pictures. Put in the correct noun in the place of the picture. Do not forget to put a preposition before the noun. Write in the blanks provided.

The first one is done as an example.

Mr. and Mrs. Smith are great writers. They rise from <u>bed</u> at 5 o'clock

in the morning. They work _____ _____ in the morning

_____ at night. They are always busy. Mrs. Smith walks

_____ from her house. Mr. Smith writes his short stories

_____ his_____. In the evening Mr. and Mrs.

Smith tell their new stories _____ _____.

They sit _____ _____ placed _____

a big _____ Some children sit _____ the _____

Some sit _____ the _____ But they all listen to the

story carefully. At the end of each story the children say "Thank you" _____

_____ .

Grammar in Quotes

Complete the following using 'before' and 'after'.

In the English alphabet, the letter S comes _____ the letter W. That is, W comes _____ S.

Now study the following quote. First make sure that you understand its meaning. Copy the two prepositions in the two blanks below the quote.

"Success comes before work only in the dictionary." (8 words)

_____ _____

Now try to learn the quote by heart. Cover the full quote with a scale or a notebook or an instrument box. Fill up the blanks with the original words, one word at a time. Try to learn at least one word at a time. Do not jump the steps.

"Success comes _____ work only in the dictionary."

"Success comes _____ work only _____ the dictionary."

"Success comes _____ work only _____ _____ dictionary."

"_____ comes _____ work only _____ _____ dictionary."

"_____ comes _____ _____ only _____ _____ dictionary."

"_____ comes _____ _____ only _____ _____ _____ ."

"_____ comes _____ _____ _____ _____ _____ _____ ."

"_____ _____ _____ _____

_____ _____ _____ ." (8 words)

EXCLAMATIONS

Revision: Types of Sentences ——————————

Answer the following questions:

1. How many types of sentences are there – two, three, four or twenty-six?

    _____

2. Name the different types of sentences.

    _____

3. Put the appropriate punctuation mark at the end of each sentence. Use the full stop (.), the question mark (?) or the exclamation mark (!).

    1. Sit down
    2. What a terrible thunder
    3. Who is the Prime Minister of India now
    4. You have an excellent teacher
    5. What an excellent teacher she is
    6. Do not clean the blackboard
    7. The eraser is made of rubber

Look at the following pictures. You can see a boy and a girl, Joe and Mary. They are Americans. Their teacher has brought them on a tour to India. Joe and Mary are wonderstruck at what they see in the different cities of India. Fill in their speech bubbles with exclamatory phrases beginning with 'What' and 'How'. Do not forget the punctuation mark.

Teacher: Yes, it is very beautiful.

Teacher: Yes, it is the biggest banyan tree in the world. It is enormous.

Teacher: Yes, it is the second longest beach in the world.

Teacher: Yes, it is a very big temple.

Teacher: Yes, it is a beautiful statue.

Teacher: Yes, it is a huge crowd.

 Points to Remember

Short exclamations (phrases) beginning with 'what' require a naming word (noun): tree, building, temple.

Short exclamations (phrases) beginning with 'how' require a describing word (adjective): tall, beautiful, big.

Grammar and I

Do exclamations express only the feeling of wonder?
No. They express other feelings, too.
Study the describing words in the list. Then react to the following situations. Put an exclamation mark (!) after filling up a blank.

lucky	unlucky	sad
terrible	cruel	kind
clever	simple	beautiful
foolish	ugly	

Situation	Your Reaction
Example: Your father has won a lottery.	How lucky!
1. You are watching a magic show. An elephant is standing on a small stool with all its four legs on it.	How _____
2. You are walking along a street. You watch a boy stealing money from a beggar.	How _____
3. You watch a man riding on a bullock cart. He is repeatedly beating the animals.	How _____
4. You have missed a lottery prize. You have missed it by just one digit.	How _____
5. You are looking at a life size picture of Mahatma Gandhi. You are looking at his clothes.	How _____
6. Your friend is adding 2 and 4. His answer is 8, not six.	How _____

Study the following pictures. Complete the exclamatory sentences. Use complete sentences to express their feelings. Follow the examples:

Situation	Exclamation using 'how'	Exclamation using 'what'
Example: Keywords: costly ice cream	How costly this ice cream is!	What a costly ice cream this is!
Report Card Math 100 100 English Keywords: perfect score		
Keywords: neatly dressed pupil		
Keywords: beautiful flowers		
Keywords: sweet cake		

Exclamations Using Plural Nouns

Study the following pictures. Decide what feelings are natural to the speakers in the situation. Complete the exclamatory sentences. Use complete sentences to express their feelings.

Note that the naming words have to be in the plural.

Situation	Sentence using 'how'	Sentence using 'what'
Example: Keywords: lovely/cats	How lovely these cats are!	What lovely cats these are!
 Keywords: funny/ characters		
 Keywords: beautiful/ colourful/flowers		
 Keywords: fast/ computers		

Grammar in Quotes

Study the following quote. Learn its meaning. Then memorise it by writing the missing words in the blanks.

"What a heavy thing the pen is!" (7 words)

"_____ a heavy thing the pen is!"

"_____ a heavy thing the pen _____!"

"_____ _____ heavy thing the pen _____!"

"_____ _____ heavy thing _____ pen _____!"

"_____ _____ heavy thing _____ _____ _____!"

"_____ _____ heavy _____ _____

_____ _____!"

"_____ _____ _____ _____ _____

_____ _____ !" (7 words)

ABSTRACT NOUNS

1. a. How many sense organs do you have? Circle the correct number.

   Two, three, four, five, six

   b. Match the action connected with the organ. Use the verbs in the following list and complete the column.

   hear, see, smell, taste, touch

Organ (Noun)	Action (Verb)
Ear	_____
Eye	_____
Nose	_____
Skin	_____
Tongue	_____

2. In how many ways can you experience these words written below? In what ways can you sense them?

   music: _____ _____ _____ _____ _____

   glass: _____ _____ _____ _____ _____

   honey: _____ _____ _____ _____ _____

   snow: _____ _____ _____ _____ _____

   ice cream: _____ _____ _____ _____ _____

   waterfalls: _____ _____ _____ _____ _____

3. Which of the following can you experience with at least one of your senses? Put an X if none of the senses can be used to experience them.

The Thing (Noun)	Hear	See	Smell	Taste	Touch	None of them
mango						
thought						
tiger						
truth						
beauty						
tree						
love						
teeth						
honesty						
speech						

Are there some nouns in the table above, which you cannot experience with any of your senses? Yes / No

Write those five nouns here:

_____ _____ _____ _____ _____

 Points to Remember

The nouns that can be felt or experienced with at least one of the senses are called concrete nouns.
Example: book, song, tea, flower
The nouns that cannot be felt or experienced with any of the senses are called abstract nouns.
Example: honesty, thought, advice, knowledge, love.

Most abstract nouns are uncountable. Most abstract nouns are used only in the singular form.

Examples: truth, charity, joy, beauty, fear, honesty, love, advice, courage, kindness, selfishness

To the teacher: Some smart students might ask, "How then do we experience or know abstract things like 'thought' and 'honesty'?" The answer is that we experience or feel or sense them with our mind or brain or heart.

COMPOSITION

Rewrite the following story. Fill the blanks with suitable abstract nouns. <u>The adjective from which you will form the abstract noun is present in the sentences before the blanks.</u> Choose appropriate verbs, too, from those given in brackets. The first one is done for you.

Elizabeth Blackwell was the first woman doctor. She was kind to animals. Her <u>kindness was</u> (is, was, were, are) widely known. She wanted coloured people to be free. She felt that _____ _____(is, was, were, are) important to everybody, black or white. Her white neighbours were cruel to the coloured people. Elizabeth often _____ (speak, spoke, spoken) about their _____.

She was always truthful. The famous writer Emerson always _____ (praise, praises, praised) Elizabeth's _____. She wanted to become a doctor. She was sad. Her _____ was due to this: no medical college accepted her as a student. In those days girls did not go to college. One day the happy news came when a medical college gave her admission. Her _____ _____

(was, is, are, were) boundless at that time.

Write in column 2 the qualities of the great men and women shown in column 1.
List of qualities:
honesty, beauty, kindness, bravery, creativity, imagination, courage

Picture	Abstract Noun
Sarojini Naidu	Honesty
Rabindra Nath Tagore	_____
Bhagat Singh	_____
Rani Laxmibai	_____
Dr. B.R. Ambedkar	_____

Common Mistakes

Rewrite the following sentences after correcting the mistakes in them. All the mistakes are to do with the abstract nouns.

1. The class teacher gives us a lot of advices.

   _____

2. I like listening to Hindustani and film musics.

   _____

3. You can still find a lot of poverties in India.

   _____

4. Good teachers give useful informations.

   _____

5. India has made a lot of progresses since 1947.

   _____

Grammar in Quotes

Underline the two abstract nouns in the following proverb.
"Honesty is the best policy." (5 words)

Find out its meaning. Then learn it by heart.

"Honesty is _____ _____ policy."

"Honesty _____ _____ _____ policy."

"_____ _____ _____ _____ policy."

"_____ _____ _____

_____ _____." (5 words)

IMPERATIVE SENTENCES

Revision

1. Fill up the following blanks. Choose the correct word from those given in brackets.

(a) Sentences can be divided broadly into _____ types. (one, two, three, four)

(b) They are:

Statements or Declarative Sentence

_____ or Interrogatives

Requests or Imperatives

_____ or Exclamatory sentences

(commands, questions, exclamations, instructions)

🔍 Points to Remember

An imperative sentence is an order or instruction or request. It always begins with a verb.

Stand up!	=	You stand up!
Sit down!	=	You sit down!
Speak up!	=	You speak up!

'You' is often omitted

An order can be changed into a request by
(a) adding 'please'
(b) changing the sentence into a question and adding please
(c) changing the loudness and tone of the speech.

Order/Instructions	Request	Request
Put the book down!	Please put the book down.	Could you please put the book down?
	Put the book down, please.	Could you put the book down, please?
Pass the notebooks!	Please pass the notebooks.	Could you please pass the notebooks?
	Pass the notebooks, please.	Could you pass the notebooks, please?

Order/Instructions	Request	Request
Stop talking!	Please stop talking. Stop talking, please.	Could you please stop talking? Could you stop talking, please?
Don't make a noise!	Please don't make a noise. Don't make a noise, please.	Could you please stop making a noise? Could you stop making a noise, please?

Change the following orders into requests.

(a) Come in!

(b) Stop chatting!

(c) Write down the proverbs!

(d) Clean the blackboard immediately!

(e) Bring the progress card at once!

(f) Do the exercise now!

Change the following into orders.

(a) Please do not disturb me.

(b) Could you please speak up?

(c) Please get your mother's signature here.

(d) Could you shut the door, please?

(e) Can you all pick up the litter?

(f) Please do not spit here.

Instructions given by the police or the army are orders.

Example: Platoon, right turn!

              Or

Group, forward march!

Blind Shots

Step One: The teacher asks students in the first row not to turn back. They should try to remember who sits where. The teacher may test their ability to remember the names and positions of the students sitting in the last row or last but one row or both.

Step Two: First, the aim must be set.

Examples:

To clean the backboard.

To empty the dustbin.

To hand homework notebook to teacher.

To shake hands with X.

To lend a pen or pencil or eraser to Y.

Step Three: The teacher then asks the whole class to prepare the orders necessary to achieve the aim. The students in the front rows are told to call the students sitting behind by their names and then give the orders.

Example:

Aim: To clean blackboard.

Orders: X and Y in the last row, stand up!

       Go to the blackboard.

       Collect a/the duster.

       Use a piece of cloth or a sheet of paper.

       Clean the blackboard.

The orders will be carried out by those in the last few rows. All students should write down the orders.

Rule 1: Before giving the order, name the student who has to carry out the order. If a second order is given to the same person, use 'You' instead of his/her name.

Rule 2: The orders should be complete, clear and loud enough, so that everyone can hear them. For example, if the order "Get a duster!" is not heard, cleaning cannot be done.

Rule 3: The teacher will decide whether the orders are clear, complete and loud enough.

You don't have to shout. Even a whisper can be effective, if the class is quiet.

Rule 4: Only one person should speak at a time.

> **To the teacher:** The commandants' success will depend on the number and kind of their orders and also on the faithfulness with which the orders are carried out. Highlight these aspects to the students.

Scoring: Points will be given for the following:

If the sentence is grammatically correct – 2 points

If it is spoken loud enough for everybody to hear – 1 point

If it achieves the aim – 2 points

Imperative: Instructions

Sometimes, we are given instructions by our parents, teachers and others. For example, the Geometry teacher or Art teacher may give the following instructions:

Example:

1. Draw a horizontal line from A to B. Connect B and C with a straight line. Draw a sleeping line from C to D.

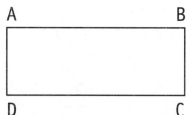

2. Draw a big rectangle. On top of it put a triangle. Draw a door. Now, you have a picture of a house.

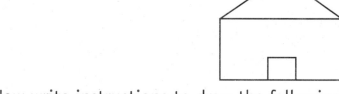

Now write instructions to draw the following figures. Follow the example.

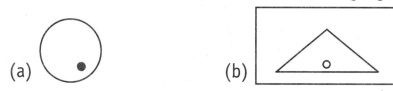

(a)   (b)

Orders can be changed into instructions for teaching or social purposes by the way in which they are spoken.

Learn to make Chocolate Today

Your friend wants to learn how to make chocolate. You are going to teach your friend to do that. The list of items needed to make chocolate is given below. The steps and the action words required are also given.

Ingredients

condensed milk	250 gm
butter	150 gm
sugar	¾ cup
cocoa powder	¼ cup
nuts	½ cup

Procedure:

1. Getting ingredients ready
2. Getting vessels ready
3. Pouring condensed milk into a pan
4. Adding butter to the milk
5. Placing the pan on a stove
6. Lighting the stove carefully
7. Stirring the milk and butter mixture
8. Adding the sugar, cocoa, and nuts
9. Stirring the mixture
10. Keeping an eye on the clock
11. Noting the time
12. Turning the stove off after 15 minutes
13. Emptying hot chocolate into a tray
14. Cutting hot chocolate into pieces
15. Putting the chocolate tray into the fridge

Write down the instructions to your friend in the space given below. Use only imperative sentences. First, write a rough copy. Ask people at home/your teacher to check it. Then write the final version.

Example, the first three instructions can be:

1. Get all the ingredients ready: condensed milk 250 gm, butter 150 gm, sugar ¾ cup, cocoa powder ¼ cup and nuts ½ cup.

2. Get all the vessels ready.

3. Pour condensed milk into a pan.

4. _____

5. _____

6. _____

7. _____

8. _____

9. _____

10. _____

To the teacher: Make this exercise appropriate to your class. You may reduce the number of sentences in the procedure by deleting the non-essential specifications and repetitions. Point out the possibilities of using 'and'. Add adverbs such as 'gently', 'slowly', carefully', 'neatly' and 'quickly' to some of the sentences.

Making Ginger Tea

Your partner wants to make ginger tea for five people. He/she has all ingredients. Use the procedure given below and dictate instructions to your friend on how to make ginger tea. Remember to choose only 10 important instructions. Then write the dictated sentences in the space given below.

Tea dust	5 spoons
Sugar	5 spoons
Water	3 cups
Milk	2 cups
Ginger juice	1 spoon

1. Getting all the ingredients ready
2. Getting the pan ready
3. Pouring the water into the pan
4. Pouring the milk too into the pan
5. Putting the pan on the stove
6. Lighting the stove
7. Putting the tea dust into the water-milk mixture
8. Allowing the mixture to boil
9. Keeping an eye on the clock
10. Switching the stove off after 2 minutes
11. Pouring the tea through a strainer
12. Pouring the tea into the cups
13. Putting a few drops of ginger juice into the tea.

Dictated instructions:

1. _____

_____

2. _____

_____

3. _____

   _____

4. _____

   _____

5. _____

   _____

6. _____

   _____

7. _____

   _____

8. _____

   _____

9. _____

   _____

10. _____

   _____

Now you and your partner should check the dictated sentences. Correct them if necessary.

Recall

1. What is an imperative sentence?

   An imperative sentence is one of the _____ (1, 2, 3, 4, 5,) types of sentences.

2. In imperative sentences, a _____ (verb/noun/adverb/adjective) starts the sentence.

3. Imperative sentences can be _____, or instructions, or

   _____

COMPOSITION

Imagine that you are Aladdin. Today is your mother's birthday. You want to give her hot vegetable biryani/pulao, a fruit salad made from uncommon fruits, and hot tea. You have your mother's maid to help you and a Genie to carry out your orders. Complete the following dialogue. The word list contains all the verbs, nouns and adverbs you will need to complete the dialogue.

Word List

verbs	nouns	adverbs
is	plates	well
get	cups	
wash	spoons	
clean	fruits	
keep	apples	
warm	pineapples	
heat	mangoes	
make	pears	
light	milk	
thank	honey	
	jelly	
	mistakes	

Alladin (you): Genie

Genie: Yes, master.

Alladin: _____ some vegetable biryani.

Genie: Yes, master (he disappears).

Alladin: Aya, please _____ all the _____

      Also _____ the knives _____

Genie: Here you are, master. (gives you a plate of biryani)

Alladin: But this _____ cold.

      Aya, can you _____ it, please?

Genie: What next, master?

Alladin: Get me some _____ .

Genie: What fruits?

Alladin: Get some _____, some _____, some _____, and some _____.

Genie: What else?

Alladin: Bring some _____ and a cake.

Genie: Yes, Master (he disappears).

Alladin: Aya, please _____ the plates, bowls, _____, and _____ on the table.

Genie: (reappears): Sorry master I forgot to bring honey.

Alladin: Don't _____ such a _____ again.

Genie: No, I won't master.

Alladin: Oh, I forgot about the tea.

Genie: Did you call me back, master?

Alladin: Yes bring some _____ also. (Genie disappears.)

Alladin: Aya, please _____ the stove.

Genie: Here you are, master.

Alladin: Good. _____ you.

Alladin: But the _____ _____ is cold. Aya, please _____ it.

> **To the teacher:** The dialogue writing can be done in groups of three. After each group completes the dialogue they may be asked to take roles and read their parts in the class.

Grammar in Quotes

1. Study the following quote. Listen to your teacher's explanation.

Part I   "Ask not what your country can do for you."
Part II   "Ask what you can do for your country."

2. Now memorise the first part.

"Ask not what your country can do for you." (9 words)

Cover the quote with a ruler or a book. Fill up the blanks.

" _____ not what your country can do for you."

" _____ not what _____ _____ can do for you."

" _____ _____ what _____ _____ can do for you."

" _____ what _____ _____ can _____ for _____."

" _____ _____ _____ _____ _____ can _____ for _____."

" _____ _____ _____ _____ _____ _____

_____ _____ for _____."

" _____ _____ _____ _____ _____

_____ _____ _____ _____."

3. Now compare the first part with the second part of the quote.

(a) Write down the first part above the second part here:

"
_____ _____ _____ _____ _____ _____ _____ _____

_____ _____ _____."

"Ask what you can do for your country."

(b) Which word is found in part I but not in Part II?

4. Part II can be easily learnt by heart, because it is very much like Part I.

5. Re-read Part II. Write Part II five times here.

"
_____ _____ _____ _____ _____ _____

_____ _____ _____ _____." (8 words)

"
_____ _____ _____ _____

_____ _____ _____ _____." (8 words)

"
_____ _____ _____ _____

_____ _____ _____ _____." (8 words)

"
_____ _____ _____ _____

_____ _____ _____ _____." (8 words)

"
_____ _____ _____ _____

_____ _____ _____ _____." (8 words)

Fill up the blanks:

Both parts of the quotes are _____ sentences (interrogative,

imperative, declarative, exclamatory), because both parts _____

(end, begin) with a verb.

ANSWERS

Word Building
Prefixes

Part of the Word		+ Full Word
1. unwise	un	+ wise
2. unpleasant	un	+ pleasant
3. unsatisfactory	un	+ satisfactory
4. discomfort	dis	+ comfort
5. disobey	dis	+ obey
6. impossible	im	+ possible
7. impatient	im	+ patient
8. imperfect	im	+ perfect
9. unlucky	un	+ lucky
10. inaccurate	in	+ accurate
11. incorrect	in	+ correct
12. insincere	in	+ sincere
13. unhappy	un	+ happy

Which of the following is the meaning of 'pre-'? Ring the meaning.

Always, **before**, after, central

(a)	happy	x	unhappy
	wise	x	unwise
	loving	x	unloving
	natural	x	unnatural
	known	x	unknown
(b)	prove	x	disprove
	obey	x	disobey
	like	x	dislike
	please	x	displease
	connect	x	disconnect
(c)	possible	x	impossible
	polite	x	impolite
	patient	x	impatient
	proper	x	improper
	perfect	x	imperfect
(d)	correct	x	incorrect
	direct	x	indirect
	decent	x	indecent
	dependent	x	independent
	expensive	x	inexpensive

(e) 1. Take this magical drink. You will become invisible.
2. Nothing is impossible with hard work.
3. Some diseases are incurable.
4. Some kings are unwise.
5. Some people are unlucky.
6. This eraser is uncommon.

Suffixes

In all the sentences marked 'a', the underlined words are adjectives. Because they add to the meaning of <u>nouns</u>. Look at the sentences marked 'b'. All the underlined words in them are adverbs. Because they add to the meaning of <u>verbs</u>.

Spelling Rule: 1

speedy	speedily
lazy	lazily
cozy	cozily

Spelling Rule: 2

Now turn the following adjectives into their adverbs:

able	ably
probable	probably
single	singly
possible	possibly
gentle	gently

Spelling Rule: 3

verbs	noun
reduce	reduction
produce	production

Spelling Rule: 4

Create more nouns from the following verbs by adding 'tion' or '-ion'

Verb		Noun
revise	_	revision
rotate	_	rotation
relate	_	relation
deduce	_	deduction
promote	_	promotion
duplicate	_	duplication
devote	_	devotion
supervise	_	supervision

Create your own nouns from the following verbs:

act	–	action
exhibit	–	exhibition
connect	–	connection
insert	–	insertion
protect	–	protection
subtract	–	subtraction

Suffix '-ment'

Make the noun forms from the following verbs using '-ment'.

manage	management
postpone	postponement
govern	government
imprison	imprisonment
amaze	amazement
discourage	discouragement
encourage	encouragement
develop	development
judge	judgement

Activity

Thomas Alva Edison

'-ment'	'-ly'	'-tion'	'-ion'
amazement	carefully	invention	decision
excitement	patiently	observation	
disappointment	warmly		
	eagerly		

Grammar in Quotes

Study the following proverb. Spot the opposite with a prefix.

'What is done cannot be undone.'

Done – Undone (write three times)

Of the following mistakes that one may commit, which are the ones that can be rectified?

Both

Fill in the missing words in the proverb:

"What is done cannot be undone." (6 words)

"What is done cannot be undone."

"What is done cannot be undone."

"What is done cannot be undone."

"What is done cannot be undone."

"What is done cannot be undone." (6 words)

Countable and Uncountable Nouns

Revision: Nouns and Articles

1. What is a noun?

A noun is a naming word. It is a person, a place, an animal or a thing.

2. Ring the nouns in the following sentences:

Computers are now made in India.

Some boys run fast.

Some girls run fast, too.

3. Underline the articles in the following sentences:

An apple a day keeps the doctor away.

A bird in hand is better than two in the bush.

The dog wags its tail.

Fill up the blanks with the correct number.

four bananas	one rose	bagful of rice
bagful of salt	four pencils	four cats
one monkey	five penguins	a lot of water

Were you able to count the things in all the pictures above?

No

Fill up the blanks with uncountable nouns.

lead

1. Most Indians use gold to make ornaments. Only some Indians, for example, the Lambadis of Andhra Pradesh use lead to make ornaments.

2. India produces enough food. Its stock of wheat and rice is excellent. It produces a lot of milk because of its high cattle population.

3. Using straw, grass and wood, India produces its own paper. It produces pencils using wood and graphite.

4. India produces enough wool to make sweaters for its people. In Kancheepuram, Benaras and other places Indians use silk to make sarees. In most places, cotton is used to make sarees. But sarees made from silk are very expensive and very beautiful.

5. Before <u>plastic</u> was invented, furniture was made of <u>wood</u> and steel all over the world. Now we have plastic chairs, plastic tables and plastic stands. India produces enough <u>plastic</u> to make these things. Using <u>rubber</u>, we also make tyres and tubes. Like Malaysia, India grows a lot of rubber trees.

Common Mistakes

Rewrite the sentences after correcting the mistakes in them.

1. All India Radio gives us news.
2. We have five chairs at home.
3. They use a lot of furniture.
4. He eats two mangoes a day.
5. I eat different fruits in different seasons.
6. Some vegetarians eat chicken.
7. These five fish are of the same kind.
8. Our uniforms are made of two pieces of cloth.
9. I have thirty pieces of jewellery, including these five rings and bangles.
10. The exhibition gives much information.

Composition

Fill up the following blanks with 'a' 'an' 'the' or 'X'. Put 'X' if none of the three articles can be used.

<u>X</u> Paper was first made about five hundred years ago. Before that some people wrote with <u>an</u> iron rod on slabs made of clay. <u>The</u> paper you are using now is made from <u>X</u> wood. <u>The</u> paper used to make currency notes is of a very special kind. <u>X</u> Ink too was invented about five hundred years ago. <u>The</u> ink we put into <u>a</u> ball point pen is different from <u>the</u> ink we put into <u>a</u> fountain pen. Invisible inks are made from <u>an</u> oil extracted from a plant. <u>X</u> Indelible ink is <u>the</u> ink that cannot be erased. Ink is very useful because it helps us spread knowledge. This is why <u>a</u> famous writer has said, "<u>A</u> drop of <u>X</u> ink can make millions think".

Composition
FURNITURE SHOP

Describe four things in the shop to your friend. While describing you can state:
Now begin:

1. There is a <u>sofa</u> in the shop.
   It is in the middle of the shop.
   It is made of wood and cloth.
2. There is a chair in the shop.
   It is in the left hand corner of the shop.
   It is made of wood.
3. There is a table in the shop.
   It is in the middle of the shop, in front of the sofa.
   It is made of wood. It has a round shape.
4. There is a dressing table in the shop.
   It is on the right hand side of the shop.
   It has a mirror on it. It is made of wood.

Grammar in Quotes

"Blood is thicker than water."

1. Now, underline the two nouns in it.

<u>blood</u>   <u>water</u>

Are they both countable or uncountable?
They both are uncountable.

2. Learn the proverb by heart.

"Blood <u>is</u> thicker than water."
"Blood <u>is</u> thicker <u>than</u> water."
"Blood <u>is</u> <u>thicker</u> <u>than</u> water."
"Blood <u>is</u> <u>thicker</u> <u>than</u> <u>water</u>."
"<u>Blood</u> <u>is</u> <u>thicker</u> <u>than</u> <u>water</u>." (5 words)

Prepositions
Revision

1. Ring the preposition in the following list of words.

   (under,) the, your, put

2. Which word in the following sentence is a preposition? Underline the preposition.

   "Don't leave your shoes <u>on</u> the sofa!"

3. What is the meaning of 'pre-' in 'preposition'? Circle your answer.

always, (before,) after, now

1.b. Look at the eight words underlined in the poem. Three of them are not prepositions. Circle only the prepositions.

Ans: in, on, upon.

2. Group the prepositions that are underlined in the following sentences. Put them in two groups and write them in the table given below:

Prepositions of Position	Prepositions of Direction
on	to
on	to
in	from
into	to
under	from
between	to

3. Fill the blanks in the following text choosing the correct preposition.

The policemen and a thief are standing on the top shelf. On the next shelf, a frog is sitting with a baby frog. Dinky, the clever mouse, is hiding under the shelf. Kitty, the cat, is sitting in a basket.

Fill up the blanks in the following sentences with prepositions of time.

1. All Fools' Day is celebrated on 1 April.

2. The Mumbai – Delhi Rajdhani Express leaves at 5 p.m.

3. Penicillin was discovered in 1928.

4. The first T.V was made in 1927.

5. India got its freedom at 12 o'clock mid night.

6. In some parts of the world the sun sets very early, at 3 p.m.

7. In some other parts of the world the sun sets very late, at 8 p.m.

8. We celebrate Christmas in December.

9. The first atom bomb exploded at 8.15 a.m. on 6 August in the year 1945.

10. India won the World cup in hockey in 1975.

Common Mistakes

Put the correct prepositions in the place of the incorrect ones:

1. The child sat in the stool.
   The child sat on the stool.

2. I go to school from the school bus.
   I go to school by the school bus.

3. I will meet you on 5 o'clock.
   I will meet you at 5 o'clock.

4. There is too much hair in his face.
   There is too much hair on his face.

5. Place these coloured glasses in your eyes. You can then see the eclipse clearly.
   Place these coloured glasses on your eyes. You can then see the eclipse clearly.

6. I want to see a new Hindi play in the theatre.
   I want to see a new Hindi play at the theatre.

Composition

Mr. and Mrs. Smith are great writers. They rise from bed at 5 o'clock in the morning. They work from nine in the morning to seven at night. They are always busy. Mrs. Smith walks to office from her house. Mr. Smith writes his short stories on his desk. In the evening Mr. And Mrs. Smith tell their new stories to children. They sit on chairs placed around a big table. Some children sit on the sofa. Some sit on the floor. But they all listen to the story carefully. At the end of each story the children say "Thank you" to them.

Grammar in Quotes

In the English alphabet, the letter S comes before the letter W. That is, W comes after S. Two preposition are:

before   in

"Success comes before work only in the dictionary."
"Success comes before work only in the dictionary."
"Success comes before work only in the dictionary."
"Success comes before work only in the dictionary."
"Success comes before work only in the dictionary."
"Success comes before work only in the dictionary."
"Success comes before work only in the dictionary."
"Success comes before work only in the dictionary."
(8 words)

Exclamations

Revision: Types of Sentences

Answer the following questions:

1. How many types of sentences are there – two, three, four or twenty-six?
   There are four types of sentences.

2. Name the different types of sentences.
   Declarative, interrogative, exclamatory, and imperative.

3. Put the appropriate punctuation mark at the end of each sentence. Use the full stop (.), the question mark (?) or the exclamation mark (!).

1. Sit down.
2. What a terrible thunder!
3. Who is the Prime Minister of India now?
4. You have an excellent teacher.
5. What an excellent teacher she is!
6. Do not clean the blackboard.
7. The eraser is made of rubber.

1. What a beauty!
2. What a tree!
3. What a beach!
4. How big!
5. How beautiful!
6. How huge!

Grammar and I

1. How sad!
2. How terrible!
3. How cruel!
4. How unlucky!
5. How simple!
6. How foolish!

Exclamation using 'how'	Exclamation using 'what'
How perfect this score is!	What a perfect score this is!
How neatly dressed this pupil is!	What a neatly dressed pupil this is!
How beautiful these flowers are!	What beautiful flowers these are!
How sweet this cake is!	What a sweet cake this is!

Exclamations Using Plural Nouns

Sentence using 'how'	Sentence using 'what'
How funny these characters are!	What funny characters these are!
How beautiful and colourful these flowers are!	What beautiful and colourful flowers these are!
How fast these computers are!	What fast computers these are!

Grammar in Quotes

"What a heavy thing the pen is!"
"What a heavy thing the pen is!"
"What a heavy thing the pen is!"
"What a heavy thing the pen is!"
"What a heavy thing the pen is!"
"What a heavy thing the pen is!"
"What a heavy thing the pen is!" (7 words)

Abstract Nouns

1. a. How many sense organs do you have? Circle the correct number.

Two, three, four, (five,) six

b. Match the action connected with the organ.

Organ (Noun)	Action (Verb)
Ear	hear
Eye	see
Nose	smell
Skin	touch
Tongue	taste

2. music: hear
   glass: see, touch
   honey: see, touch, taste, smell
   snow: see, touch, taste
   ice cream: see, touch, taste, smell
   waterfalls: see, hear, touch

3. Which of the following can you experience with at least one of your senses? Put an X if none of the senses can be used to experience them.

The Thing (Noun)	Hear	See	Smell	Taste	Touch	None of them
mango		see	smell	taste	touch	
thought						X
tiger		see			touch	
truth						X
beauty						X
tree		see			touch	
love						X
teeth		see			touch	
honesty						X
speech	hear					

Are there some nouns in the table above, which you cannot experience with any of your senses?

Yes.

Write those five nouns here:

thought, truth, beauty, love, honesty.

Composition

Rewrite the following story. Fill the blanks with suitable abstract nouns.

Elizabeth Blackwell was the first woman doctor. She was kind to animals. Her kindness was widely known. She wanted coloured people to be free. She felt that freedom was important to everybody, black or white. Her white neighbours were cruel to the coloured people. Elizabeth often spoke about their cruelty. She was always truthful. The famous writer Emerson always praised Elizabeth's truthfulness. She wanted to become a doctor. She was sad. Her sadness was due to this: no medical college accepted her as a student. In those days girls did not go to college. One day the happy news came when a medical college gave her admission. Her happiness was boundless at that time.

Write in column 2 the qualities of the great men and women shown in column 1.

Picture	Abstract Noun
Rabindra Nath Tagore	creativity
Bhagat Singh	courage
Rani Laxmibai	bravery
Dr. B.R. Ambedkar	kindness

Common Mistakes

Rewrite the following sentences after correcting the mistakes in them.

1. The class teacher gives us a lot of advice.
2. I like listening to Hindustani and film music.
3. You can still find a lot of poverty in India.
4. Good teachers give useful information.
5. India has made a lot of progress since 1947.

Grammar in Quotes

Underline the two abstract nouns in the following proverb.

"Honesty is the best policy." (5 words)

Find out its meaning. Then learn it by heart.

"Honesty is <u>the</u> <u>best</u> policy."
"Honesty <u>is</u> <u>the</u> <u>best</u> policy."
"<u>Honesty</u> <u>is</u> <u>the</u> <u>best</u> policy."
"<u>Honesty</u> <u>is</u> <u>the</u> <u>best</u> <u>policy</u>." (5 words)

Imperative Sentences

1. a. Sentences can be divided broadly into <u>four</u> types.

b. They are:

Statements or Declarative Sentence

<u>Questions</u> or Interrogatives

Requests or Imperatives

<u>Exclamations</u> or Exclamatory sentences

Change the following orders into requests.

(a) Please come in.

Come in, please.

Could you please come in?

(b) Please stop chatting.

Stop chatting, please.

Could you please stop chatting?

(c) Please write down the proverbs.

Write down the proverbs, please.

Could you please write down the proverbs?

(d) Please clean the blackboard immediately.

Clean the blackboard immediately, please.

Could you please clean the blackboard immediately?

(e) Please bring the progress card at once.

Bring the progress card at once, please.

Could you please bring the progress card at once?

(f) Please do the exercise now.

Do the exercise now, please.

Could you please do the exercise now?

Change the following into orders.

(a) Do not disturb me.

(b) Speak up.

(c) Get your mother's signature here.

(d) Shut the door.

(e) Pick up the litter.

(f) Do not spit here.

Write instructions to draw the figures.

(a) Draw a circle. At the right side of the circle and inside it, draw a dot.

(b) Draw a rectangle. Draw a triangle inside it. Draw a small circle inside the triangle.

Learn to make Chocolate Today

Write down the instructions to your friend.

1. Get all the ingredients ready: condensed milk 250 gm, butter 150 gm, sugar ¾ cup, cocoa powder ¼ cup and nuts ½ cup.
2. Get all the vessels ready.
3. Pour condensed milk into a pan.
4. Add butter to the milk.
5. Place the pan on a stove.
6. Light the stove carefully.
7. Stir the milk and butter mixture.
8. Add the sugar, cocoa, and nuts.
9. Stir the mixture.
10. Keep an eye on the clock.
11. Note the time.
12. Turn the stove off after 15 minutes.
13. Empty hot chocolate into a tray.
14. Cut hot chocolate into pieces.
15. Put the chocolate tray into the fridge.

Activity

Making Ginger Tea

Dictated instructions:

1. Get all the ingredients ready: tea dust 5 spoons, sugar 5 spoons, water 3 cups, milk 2 cups, and ginger juice 1 spoon.
2. Pour the water into the pan.
3. Pour the milk too into the pan.
4. Put the pan on the stove.
5. Put the tea dust into the water-milk mixture.
6. Allow the mixture to boil.
7. Switch the stove off after two minutes.
8. Pour the tea through a strainer.
9. Pour the tea into the cups.
10. Put a few drops of ginger juice into the tea.

Recall

1. What is an imperative sentence?

   An imperative sentence is one of the <u>4</u> (four) types of sentences.

2. In imperative sentences, a <u>verb</u> (verb/noun/ adverb/adjective) starts the sentence.

3. Imperative sentences can be <u>requests</u>, or instructions, or <u>orders</u>.

Composition

Alladin (you): Genie

Genie: Yes, master.

Alladin: <u>Get</u> some vegetable biryani.

Genie: Yes, master (he disappears).

Alladin: Aya, please <u>wash</u> all the <u>plates</u>.
          Also <u>clean</u> the knives <u>well</u>.

Genie: Here you are, master. (gives you a plate of biryani)

Alladin: But this <u>is</u> cold.
          Aya, can you <u>heat</u> it, please.

Genie: What next, master?

Alladin: Get me some <u>fruits</u>.

Genie: What fruits?

Alladin: Get some <u>apples</u>, some <u>mangoes</u>, some <u>pineapples</u>, and some <u>pears</u>.

Genie: What else?

Alladin: Bring some <u>honey</u> and a cake.

Genie: Yes, master (he disappears).

Alladin: Aya, please <u>keep</u> the plates, bowls, <u>cups</u>, and <u>spoons</u> on the table.

Genie: (reappears): Sorry master I forgot to bring honey.

Alladin: Don't <u>make</u> such a <u>mistake</u> again.

Genie: No, I won't master.

Alladin: Oh, I forgot about the tea.

Genie: Did you call me back, master?

Alladin: Yes, bring some <u>jelly</u> also. (Genie disappears.)

Alladin: Aya, please <u>light</u> the stove.

Genie: Here you are, master.

Alladin: Good. <u>Thank</u> you.

Alldin: But the <u>milk</u> is cold. Aya, please <u>warm</u> it.

Grammar in Quotes

2. "<u>Ask</u> not what your country can do for you." (9 words)

   "<u>Ask</u> not what <u>your</u> <u>country</u> can do for you."
   "<u>Ask</u> <u>not</u> what <u>your</u> <u>country</u> can do for you."
   "<u>Ask</u> <u>not</u> what <u>your</u> <u>country</u> can <u>do</u> for you."
   "<u>Ask</u> <u>not</u> <u>what</u> <u>your</u> <u>country</u> can <u>do</u> for <u>you</u>."
   "<u>Ask</u> <u>not</u> <u>what</u> <u>your</u> <u>country</u> can <u>do</u> for <u>you</u>."
   "<u>Ask</u> <u>not</u> <u>what</u> <u>your</u> <u>country</u> <u>can</u> <u>do</u> <u>for</u> <u>you</u>."

3. a. Write down the first part above the second part here:

   "<u>Ask</u> <u>not</u> <u>what</u> <u>your</u> <u>country</u> <u>can</u> <u>do</u> <u>for</u> <u>you</u>."

   "Ask what you can do for your country."

   b. Which word is found in part I but not in Part II?

   The word 'not'.

Fill up the blanks:

Both parts of the quotes are <u>imperative</u> sentences because both parts <u>begin</u> with a verb.

ENGLISH GRAMMAR

Phonics First

Phonics First Book 1
81-7693-115-2

Phonics First Book 2
81-7693-116-0

Phonics First Book 3
81-7693-117-9

Phonics First Book 4
81-7693-118-7

Phonics First Book 5
81-7693-119-5

Phonics First Book 6
81-7693-120-9

First Grammar Workbook

First Grammar Workbook 1
978817693564-7

First Grammar Workbook 2
978817693565-4

First Grammar Workbook 3
978817693566-1

Comprehension and Cloze

Comprehension & Cloze
Book 1
978817693595-1

Comprehension & Cloze
Book 2
978817693596-8

Comprehension & Cloze
Book 3
978817693597-5

Grammar Workbooks

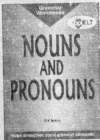
Nouns and Pronouns
978817693650-7

Articles and Conjunctions
978817693651-4

Adjectives and Adverbs
978817693652-1

Verbs 'Be' and Prepositions
978817693653-8